SCHUMANN

KREISLERIANA OPUS 16 FOR THE PIANO

EDITED BY CHARLES TIMBRELL

AN ALFRED MASTERWORK EDITION

Copyright © 2016 by Alfred Music
All rights reserved.   Printed in USA.
ISBN-10: 1-4706-3616-6
ISBN-13: 978-1-4706-3616-6

Cover art: Two Men Contemplating the Moon
(ca. 1825–1830) by Caspar David Friedrich
(German, 1774–1840), Oil on canvas

ROBERT SCHUMANN

Contents

Kreisleriana, Op. 16
Edited by Charles Timbrell

Foreword

ABOUT THIS EDITION

The autograph and the publishers' source-scores of Schumann's *Kreisleriana* are not extant. For this reason, the primary sources used in the preparation of this edition include the following:

- The **second edition** (the primary source), published in Leipzig in August 1850 by Friedrich Whistling (pl. no. 559; Schumann's personal copy at the Robert-Schumann-Haus, Zwickau, Germany)

- The **first edition**, published in Vienna in September 1838 by Tobias Haslinger (pl. no. 7570; copy at the Library of Congress, Washington, D.C.)

Secondary sources include the following:

- The **third edition**, published in Leipzig ca. 1858 by Gustav Heinze (pl. no. G. H. 18; copy at the British Library)

- **Editions by Clara Schumann**

  ° *Robert Schumann: Werke*, Series VII, Vol. 3. Edited by Clara Schumann. Leipzig: Breitkopf & Härtel, 1887 ("*Gesamtausgabe*"). Reprinted in *Piano Music of Robert Schumann*, Series I. New York: Dover Publications, 1972.

  ° *Robert Schumann: Klavier-Werke, Instructive Ausgabe*, Vol. 3. Edited by Clara Schumann. Leipzig: Breitkopf & Härtel, 1887.

  ° *Robert Schumann: Complete Piano Works*, Vol. 3. Edited by Clara Schumann. New York: Kalmus, ca. 1900 (instructive edition).

The present edition is based on the 1850 second edition, which represents Schumann's final wishes. Detailed comparisons with the first edition are given in the "Endnotes" section beginning on page 53. Several comparisons with the other editions are included as footnotes.

These sources have been compared with later editions by Harold Bauer (Schirmer, 1945), Hans Bischoff (Steingräber, 1888), Wolfgang Boetticher (Henle, 1977), Alfred Cortot (Salabert, 1946), Alfred Dörffel (Peters, ca. 1882), Enoch and Sons (1880), Gabriel Fauré (Durand, 1917), Ernst Herttrich (Henle, 2004), Hans Otto Hiekel (Henle, 1970), Alexis Hollaender (Schlesinger, 1887), Karl Klindworth (S. Lucas, ca. 1885), Hans Joachim Köhler (Peters, 1975), Conrad Kühner (Litolff, n.d.), Ignace Paderewski (The University Society, 1901), Ernst Pauer (Augener, 1881), Raoul Pugno (Librairie des Annales, 1911), Anton Rubinstein (Jurgenson, ca. 1872), Emil von Sauer (Peters, n.d.), Gino Tagliapietra (Ricordi, 1948), Otto Thümer (Augener, 1907), Max Vogrich (Schirmer, 1894), Carlo Zecchi (Curci, 1951), and Agnes Zimmermann (Novello, 1893).

Editorial Considerations

Pedaling indications in this edition are editorial unless indicated otherwise. Schumann did indicate *Ped.* markings at the beginning of each piece in *Kreisleriana*, as well as at the beginning of some sections, to imply that the damper pedal is to be used at the discretion of the performer. (The specific editorial pedaling is used in lieu of these general *ped.* indications in this edition.) Specific pedaling given by Schumann that differs from the editorial suggestions has been marked with *ped.* in parentheses and has been footnoted. Performers should ultimately base their pedaling decisions on the sonority of the piano and the acoustics of the performance venue.

Parentheses have been used in this edition (1) to identify musical elements that are believed to have been inadvertently omitted from the first and second editions (such as missing *a tempo* indications, staccato markings, etc.); (2) to clarify ambiguous or confusing dynamic indications by the composer; and (3) to show which hand may omit notes when the hands play overlapping notes (in unison). Any necessary clarification has been given in footnotes.

Metronome markings are editorial and given in parentheses. Schumann's only metronome markings, for Nos. *IV* and *VI*, are cited in footnotes for those pieces.

Clara Schumann's metronome markings, given in her *Instructive Ausgabe*, are of particular interest and are listed here:

I: Äusserst bewegt: ♩ = 104

II: Sehr innig und nicht zu rasch: ♩ = 72
          Intermezzo I: ♩ = 96
          Intermezzo II: ♩ = 112

III: Sehr aufgeregt: ♩ = 112
          Etwas langsamer: ♩ = 92

IV: Sehr langsam: ♪ = 66
          Bewegter: ♩ = 69

V: Sehr lebhaft: ♩ = 160

VI: Sehr langsam: ♪ = 108
          Etwas bewegter: ♪ = 132

VII: Sehr rasch: ♩ = 132

VIII: Schnell und spielend: ♩. = 100

THE GENESIS OF *KREISLERIANA*

On April 13, 1838, Robert Schumann (1810–1856) wrote his future wife, the young pianist Clara Wieck (1819–1896):

> Just think! since my last letter, I have finished another whole volume of new things. *Kreisleriana* I shall call it; you, and thought of you play the chief part, and I will dedicate it to you—yes, to you and to no-one else—then you will smile so sweetly when you find yourself in it again. — My music seems to me, just now so extraordinarily intricate with all its simplicity, [and] it speaks so entirely from the heart.[1]

Kreisleriana, Op. 16, is a cycle consisting of eight contrasting pieces composed in Leipzig between March 17, 1838, the date of the earliest known sketch, and May 3, when the composer noted in his diary, "*Kreisleriana* [in its final form] completed in four days. Completely new worlds opened up to me. The Kreisler piece in G minor and 6/8 meter with a trio in D minor composed in white heat."[2] The work belongs to one of Schumann's most creative periods, which included the *Davidsbündlertänze*, Op. 6; *Fantasiestücke*, Op. 12; *Kinderszenen*, Op. 15; the *Fantasie*, Op. 17; and the *Noveletten*, Op. 21.

The publication history is straightforward. In May 1838, Schumann began negotiations with the Viennese publisher Tobias Haslinger, sending him a manuscript copy (now lost). Haslinger mailed proof copies in July, and Schumann was able to forward one immediately to Clara, who was then performing in Dresden. On July 30, she wrote back:

> You can't believe how delighted I was; how beautiful these pieces are, so much is humorous, and then again mystic. Of course I'll have to play them over and over again in order to judge them more correctly…I am amazed at your genius, at all the new things in the pieces—and do you know what, sometimes I am actually frightened of you and think, is it possible that he is going to be your husband? At times I even feel that I might not be enough for you—but that you could still like me forever for that reason![3]

By this time, Schumann had decided that it would be unwise to dedicate the work to Clara because it might provoke her father, Friedrich Wieck, who had already sought to undermine their relationship. For this reason, he instead dedicated it to his friend and colleague Frédéric Chopin (1810–1849), whose *Ballade in F Major*, Op. 38, was dedicated to Schumann. Haslinger published *Kreisleriana* on September 8, 1838. Haslinger printed only a few hundred copies, and several months later Schumann wrote Clara, wondering if she thought that the publisher Heinrich Probst (an agent for Breitkopf & Härtel) might be interested in issuing "perhaps the *Toccata*, *Fantasiestücke*, *Sonata*, *Davidsbündlertänze* and *Kreisleriana* (the latter perhaps with different titles)."[4] But nothing came of this idea, and it was 10 years before a new edition of *Kreisleriana* was considered.

In August 1849, the Leipzig publisher Friedrich Whistling, one of Haslinger's successors, asked Schumann if he wished to make changes for a new edition. Schumann did so, sending his revisions in November and noting that they were substantial because "in my earlier days, I very often spoiled my pieces in an entirely capricious manner. This has now been completely remedied."[5] The revisions are in fact not too numerous. They include some repetitions or cuts of sections (in *Nos. I* and *II*), slight alterations of the endings (in *IV* and *V*), a few modifications of harmonies (in *II*), and the deletions of some *ritards* (in all but *I*). Specific differences between the first and second editions are discussed in the endnotes of the present edition. Whistling's edition appeared in August 1850.

In 1858, after Schumann's death, Whistling's successor Gustav Heinze published a newly engraved edition. Readings from the first edition were inserted in small type into the text of the second edition, as Clara Schumann was to do in both of her later editions. Since the Heinze edition postdates Schumann's death and introduces no new readings, it has not been considered as a primary source by the present editor.

Self-portrait of Hoffmann as Kreisler

---

1 Bertold Litzmann, *Clara Schumann: An Artist's Life*, Vol. 1, trans. Grace E. Hadow (New York: Vienna House, 1972; 1st ed. 1913), 154.

2 Robert Schumann, *Tagebücher*, Vol. 2, eds. Georg Eismann and Gerd Nauhaus (Leipzig: Deutscher Verlag für Musik, 1971–87), 55.

3 *Complete Correspondence of Clara and Robert Schumann*, Vol. 1, ed. Eva Weissweiler, trans. Hildegard Fritsch and Ronald L. Crawford (New York: Peter Lang, 1994–96), 219–20.

4 Ibid., Vol. 2, 32.

5 *Robert Schumann's Leben: Aus seinen Briefen geschildert*, Vol. 2, ed. Hermann Erler (Berlin: Ries & Erler, 1887), 104–05.

E. T. A. HOFFMANN'S KAPELLMEISTER JOHANNES KREISLER

Schumann grew up in a family devoted to literature. His father, August Schumann, was a bookseller and publisher whose firm issued pioneering pocket editions of such writers as Virgil, Chaucer, Cervantes, Moliere, Voltaire, Lord Byron, and Sir Walter Scott. Young Schumann studied Latin, French, and Greek from age six, and at 15 he founded a literary club that met monthly and featured readings from German poetry and prose. By the time he entered Leipzig University in 1828, he had immersed himself in one of his favorite authors, E. T. A. Hoffmann (1776–1822).

Hoffmann's influence on Schumann was particularly strong because he was also a composer and music critic. His *Fantasiestücke in Callots Manier* (*Fantasy Pieces in Callot's Manner*, 1814) is a collection of fantastical tales interspersed with music criticism. Thirteen of these items are grouped under the subtitle *Kreisleriana*, and they feature one of the most vivid characters in German literature, the highly eccentric composer Johannes Kreisler. Hoffmann describes him thus:

> Nature had tried a new recipe in creating him. The experiment had gone awry, for too little phlegm had been blended with an over-excitable temperament and a devastatingly inflammable imagination… Occasionally he would compose at night in the most exalted mood. Waking the friend who lived next door, he would play for him with the greatest enthusiasm everything he had written in incredible haste…But the next day the glorious composition would lie in the fire.[6]

Capricious, with a fondness for wine and haranguing friends and strangers alike, Kreisler could only shake himself out of his bad moods through music, sometimes scraping on his violin or thundering at the piano.

> One evening, Kreisler improvised for a group of friends. Wearing a little red cap and a Chinese dressing robe, he sat down at the piano and played while narrating a story about "lovely spirits with golden wings" (in the key of A major), a maiden in despair (A minor), a forest in springtime (B major), a dance over open graves (C major), and a pale ghost "with glowing red eyes and claw-like, bony fists stretching out of a ragged cloak (C minor).[7]

*E. T. A. Hoffmann
Self-Portrait*

Kreisler was also the leading character in Hoffmann's novel *Lebensansichten des Katers Murr* (*The Life and Opinions of the Tomcat Murr*, 1821), surely one of the most unusual 19th-century novels. In it, a vain tomcat named Murr decides to write his memoires and uses the pages of a biography of Kreisler as blotting paper. Later, due to a printing error, extended passages of Murr's memoires become interwoven with Kreisler's biography, resulting in an amusing double biography. Murr emerges as a confidant scholar and lover, while Kreisler appears to be a hypochondriac genius.

The literary critic Jeremy Adler has suggested that Hoffmann's book and Schumann's *Kreisleriana* share an "emotional and structural fragmentariness that points to a higher continuity, beyond conventional representation."[8] Similarly, the pianist and scholar Charles Rosen has observed that "the alternation of passion and satire [in Hoffmann's novel] must have seized Schumann's imagination, giving him, as it were, an excuse to yoke together musical ideas that seem incompatible at first sight, to change mood and expression without warning, to go directly from a lyric meditation to a strangely sinister scherzo or an outburst of rage."[9] It is no coincidence that the subtitle of *Kreisleriana* is *Fantasien* (*Fantasies*), which suggests a link not only with Hoffmann's *Fantasiestücke in Callots Manier* but also with Schumann's earlier Hoffmann-influenced piano work, the *Fantasiestücke*, Op. 12.

For many years, Kreisler was thought to have been modeled on the prolific German composer Ludwig Böhner (1787–1860). This identification was assumed by Schumann, and it was repeated in the Schumann literature for many decades. In recent years, however, this identification has been persuasively challenged, with the conclusion that Kreisler was largely an extension of Hoffmann's own personality.[10]

Clearly, pianists should become familiar with Hoffmann's genial and unpredictable character. He was an alter-ego for Schumann and later for Johannes Brahms (1833–1897), who went so far as to sign some of his early manuscripts *Joh. Kreisler junior*.

6 E. T. A. Hoffmann, *Fantasy Pieces in Callot's Manner*, trans. Joseph M. Hayse (Schenectady, NY: Union College Press, 1996), 15–16.
7 Ibid., 262–64.

8 E. T. A. Hoffmann, *The Life and Opinions of the Tomcat Murr*, trans. Anthea Bell (New York: Penguin Books, 1999), xxvii.

9 Charles Rosen, *The Romantic Generation* (Cambridge, MA: Harvard University Press, 1995), 673.

10 See *Early Letters of Robert Schumann*, trans. May Herbert (London: George Bell and Sons, 1888), 238–43. Evidence against the identification of Böhner is found in Axel Beer, "Johann Ludwig Böhner—E. T. A. Hoffmann's Kapellmeister Kreisler?" *Festschrift Christoph-Hellmut Mahling zum 65. Geburtstag* (Tutzing: Hans Schneider, 1997), 113–22; and in Beer's article "Böhner" in *Die Musik in Geschichte und Gegenwart*, 2nd ed. (Kassel: Bärenreiter, 1994).

CLARA SCHUMANN AND THE EARLY CHAMPIONS OF *KREISLERIANA*

Although the influence of E. T. A. Hoffmann's writing is undeniable, the main inspiration for *Kreisleriana* was Schumann's love for Clara, as he stated in the above-mentioned letter to her on April 13, 1838. Shortly after sending her a copy of the work, he wrote her: "Play my *Kreisleriana* sometimes! There is a very wild love in a few movements, and your life and mine and many of your looks."[11] Clara's inspiration is also recognized in a letter Schumann wrote to his former teacher Heinrich Dorn, in which he stated, "Clara has been practically the only motivation for the *Concert* [the *Sonata in F Minor*, Op. 14, known as the *Concert sans Orchestre*], the *Sonata* [*in F-sharp Minor*, Op. 11], the *Davidsbündlertänze*, *Kreisleriana* and the *Novellettes*."[12] Certainly *Kreisleriana* reflects Schumann's wide-ranging emotions during the period of his courtship of Clara, when they were often separated while she was on concert tours and when her possessive father posed many difficulties.

Clara learned portions of *Kreisleriana* as soon as she received a copy, informing Schumann that she "reveled in *Kreisleriana* once again tonight, after yearning for it so long. I can't tell you how beautiful [these pieces] are. I feel them as you've felt them."[13] At every opportunity she played some of them for friends and colleagues, including the pianists Ignaz Moscheles (1794–1870) and Louis Rakemann (1816–n.d.) and the composers Charles de Bériot (1802–1870) and Georg Otten (1806–1890). Shortly after they were married in September 1840, Schumann described his joy at hearing Clara practice the work; and in December of that year he wrote that she had played parts of it for some Danish visitors with deep understanding, "as though directly from my soul."[14]

Surprisingly, it was not until January 2, 1859 that Clara first played some of *Kreisleriana* in public. The venue was the important Gesellschaft der Musikfreunde in Vienna, where she performed (in order) *I, II, V, IV, VII,* and *VIII*. Shortly before, she wrote to Brahms:

Clara Wieck (1840)
by Johann Heinrich Schramm (1801–1865)

People here [in Vienna] have been clamoring the whole time for me to play the *Kreisleriana*. But they seem to me so unsuitable for a concert. However, I must give way, for Spina [a publisher and concert manager] says that I shall attract bigger crowds if I play them. But I shall have to make a selection.[15]

Subsequently, she gave partial performances in Zurich, Frankfurt, Hamburg, and Vienna, sometimes playing only *I, II,* and *VIII*. On January 5, 1870, she played *I, II, V, VI,* and *VIII* in Vienna, after which a critic praised her "unsurpassably beautiful performance."[16] No doubt Clara gave other performances, but there is no evidence that she ever played the entire work in public. On April 4, 1839, she wrote Schumann:

Listen Robert, won't you just once compose something brilliant, easy to understand, a complete and coherent piece without special titles, not too long and not too short? I would very much like to have something of yours that is intended for an audience.[17]

---

11 *Complete Correspondence of Clara and Robert Schumann*, 225.

12 *Robert Schumann's Leben: Aus seinen Briefen geschildert*, Vol. 1, 214.

13 *Complete Correspondence of Clara and Robert Schumann*, 291.

14 *The Marriage Diaries of Robert and Clara Schumann*, ed. Gerd Nauhaus, trans. Peter Ostwald (Boston: Northeastern University Press, 1993), 45.

15 *Letters of Clara Schumann & Johannes Brahms*, ed. Berthold Litzmann, Vol. 1 (New York: Vienna House, 1973; 1st ed. 1927), 93.

16 *Blätter für Theater, Musik und Kunst*, January 8, 1870, 8.

17 *Clara Schumann: An Artist's Life*, 311.

Clara might have been reacting to *Kreisleriana*, but it is also possible that she had in mind the *Fantasie*, Op. 17 (with its unclear form in the first movement and its slow and dreamy last movement); or the titled character pieces in the *Fantasiestücke*, Op. 12, and *Kinderszenen*, Op. 15; the *Davidsbündlertänze*, Op. 6 (with its obscure title and its references to the imaginary characters Florestan and Eusebius); or *Carnaval*, Op. 9 (with its brief and sometimes inexplicably titled pieces). We know from her many letters that she truly loved all of these works. But in this April letter she was reflecting the practical attitude of a virtuoso who was eager to win the public.

Franz Liszt (1811–1886) also had a high opinion of *Kreisleriana*, writing to his mistress Marie d'Agoult in late August 1838: "Haslinger sent me Schumann's *Kreisleriana*. It is extremely remarkable."[18] But within a few months he wrote Schumann that he felt that "*Kreisleriana* and the Fantasy are too difficult for the public to digest. I will keep them to play later on."[19] Although Liszt is not known to have performed *Kreisleriana* in public, a number of his students did, including Hans von Bülow (1830–1894), Karl Tausig (1841–1871), and Alfred Reisenauer (1863–1907); and in 1885 Liszt taught the work to the young Hungarian pianist Vilma Fritz (dates unknown) during two of his master classes in Weimar.

Sigismond Thalberg (1812–1871), one of Liszt's chief rivals, visited Schumann during his stay in Vienna in 1838 and sight-read *Kreisleriana* "with remarkable accomplishment and understanding," as Schumann noted in his diary.[20] But like Liszt, he is not known to have performed it publicly.

Brahms, on the other hand, played all or part of *Kreisleriana* in public on many occasions. Other contemporaries of Clara's who performed it included Charles-Valentin Alkan (1813–1888), Alexis Hollaender (1840–1924) who played the Berlin premiere, Otto Neitzel (1852–1920), Max Pauer (1866–1945), Anton Rubinstein (1829–1894), and Josef Wieniawski (1837–1912).

CLARA SCHUMANN'S EDITIONS

In early 1877, Breitkopf & Härtel proposed that Clara edit Schumann's complete works. After consulting with Brahms, she decided to undertake the task, but only if Brahms would assist her. Hundreds of letters attest to their work together, including the examination of as many autographs and early editions as they could obtain. Many other musicians also helped Clara, but by mutual understanding she was listed as the sole editor. The complete edition (*Gesamtausgabe*), numbering 21 volumes, appeared between 1881 and 1893. Regarding their editing of *Kreisleriana*, Brahms wrote her:

> You can depend on the third edition [by Heinze], with its readings from the old edition put in small print next to the second [edition]…Just so you can see that I have compared them (all three editions), I have made some unnecessary notes. Before you send the copy to Härtel, simply cross out things in blue, retaining what pleases you for the engraver.[21]

A close comparison of Clara's edition with Heinze's reveals very few discrepancies other than the style of typesetting. Ostensibly, both editions print Schumann's second edition, with insertions of readings from the first edition placed in small print in the text or in footnotes. But there are instances in which Clara tacitly conflates Schumann's two editions. For example, in *I*, *II*, *IV*, and *VI* she retains dynamics and tempo indications from the first edition while printing the musical text of the second. A shortcoming of the *Gesamtausgabe* is its lack of a critical commentary on the various sources and the variant readings.

Clara's *Instructive Ausgabe* of 1887, on the other hand, is of considerable interest. Undertaken at roughly the same time as she was preparing the *Gesamtausgabe*, this six-volume series is the most important of the many 19th-century editions of Schumann's piano works. As the most authoritative interpreter of her husband's music, Clara provided invaluable suggestions about tempo, expression, dynamics, phrasing, pedaling, and fingering. Unfortunately, her particular contributions are not identified as such, and after Clara's death the edition was revised by Carl Reinecke (1824–1910) and, most recently, Wilhelm Kempff (1895–1991). The American edition, first published by Kalmus around 1900, contains many disparities with the German edition of 1887.[22]

18 *Franz Liszt—Marie d'Agoult: Correspondance*, eds. Serge Gut and Jacqueline Bellas (Paris: Fayard, 2001), 343.

19 *Liszt's Briefe*, Vol. 1, ed. La Mara (Leipzig: Breitkopf & Härtel, 1893–1905), 27.

20 *Tagebücher*, 78.

21 *Letters of Clara Schumann & Johannes Brahms*, Vol. 2, 189.

22 For further details about Clara's two editions, see Nancy B. Reich, *Clara Schumann: The Artist and the Woman*, rev. ed. (Ithaca, NY: Cornell University Press, 1985), 241–47.

ABOUT THE MUSIC

The special place *Kreisleriana* held in Schumann's affections is clear from a letter he wrote to a Belgian admirer, Simonin de Sire (1800–1872): "Of my recent compositions—*Kinderszenen*, the *Fantasy*, Op. 17, *Arabesque*, *Blumenstück*, *Humoreske*, and *Kreisleriana*—I love *Kreisleriana* the most."[23]

The critic Franz Brendel (1811–1868), who succeeded Schumann as editor of the *Neue Zeitschrift für Musik*, was one of the first to fully appreciate the work. In 1845 he wrote:

> The most beautiful composition of [Schumann's early works] is perhaps *Kreisleriana*. Here everything…is expressed clearly and precisely; here the forms have gained the highest degree of transparency, and at the same time the work contains the most magnificent outpourings. I consider this work one of the most beautiful pieces of contemporary piano music, and those who do not know it are simply at a loss…The nocturnal humor [of his previous pieces] appears clarified and purified, the excess of fantasy—as far as this is possible at this stage of creativity—has been channeled in the confines of distinct musical structures.[24]

Indeed, Schumann's use of clear-cut forms and related key centers make *Kreisleriana* more homogeneous than some of his other sets of pieces. The key centers are:

I: D minor/G minor

II: B-flat major/G minor

III, *V*, and *VIII*: G minor/B-flat major

IV and *VI*: B-flat major

VII: C minor/G minor

The odd-numbered pieces are fast, rhythmic, and often tumultuous; the even-numbered ones are generally slower and more lyrical, but sometimes with contrasting sections within them.

The structure of the pieces and some performance suggestions are given below:

I   Äusserst bewegt (Very agitated) 12

In this piece in **ABA** form, the agitation of the outer sections is slightly calmed in the central section, where the main idea is inverted and the dynamics softened. Clara Schumann advised her student Adelina de Lara (1872–1961) not to play this piece too fast and to shape the melody in the **B** section with special care.[25] But Clara Schumann's own tempo of ♩ = 104, given in her *Instructive Ausgabe*, seems too fast for a good realization of the polyphony and the many slurs and accents. These details can be observed, along with the necessary excitement, at ♩ = ca. 84. Small rotations of the wrist are needed throughout, with shallow changes of pedal. In the **A** sections, the RH should provide rhythmic stability on the first and third beats and the LH should not be accented on the second and fourth beats. The rhythmic displacement should be clear, with neither hand predominant. Make the four-measure phrases clear and play the **B** section in tempo and without the una corda pedal.

23   *Robert Schumann's Leben: Aus seinen Briefen*, 191–92.

24   Franz Brendel, "Robert Schumann with Reference to Mendelssohn-Bartholdy and the Development of Modern Music in General," trans. Jürgen Thym, in *Schumann and His World*, ed. R. Larry Todd (Princeton: Princeton University Press, 1994), 323.

25   Adelina de Lara, "Clara Schumann's Teaching," *Music & Letters* XXVI/3 (1945), 146. De Lara's recording, made in 1951 at age 79 and reissued on compact disc (Pearl GEMM 9907), provides an interesting link to Clara Schumann.

II Sehr innig und nicht zu rasch (Very intimate and not too fast) 16

The form is **AB** (Intermezzo I) **AC** (Intermezzo II) **A** (varied) **A**. This piece is the longest and interpretively the most challenging in *Kreisleriana*. In the opening, Schumann seems to be speaking directly to Clara "from the heart," as he once expressed to her. In the **A** sections, the melodies (in all voices) should flow across the bar lines, and without exaggeration of the fermata signs and the *ritards*. The *sf* in measures 2 and 4 (and later) should not be exaggerated, perhaps more an agogic accent than a dynamic one. The many repeats of this opening theme should be treated with subtly different nuances each time. Careful half-pedaling will minimize blurs and partially retain some of the longer notes. In the two Intermezzos, make the imitations between the hands clear but avoid exaggerated dynamics. The intense chromaticism in measures 119–131, played with a perfect finger legato in both hands, must be expressive without adopting a slower tempo. The only really slow moments in the entire piece are the very brief ones in measures 36–37, 91–92, and 141–143.

III Sehr aufgeregt (Very agitated) 24

The form is **ABA Coda**. Tight rhythms and a light touch are needed in the restless **A** sections. Keep the RH fingers close to the keys, with a low wrist and drops of the hand on each slur. The lyrical **B** section requires subtle handling of the polyphony and very quiet accompanying 16th notes. Move the phrases without hesitations to each *sf*. There are many opportunities for coloristic nuances in measures 51–86. In the **Coda**, some of the lowest notes in the LH can be held with the sostenuto pedal. Many performers double the tempo beginning at measure 146, but it seems preferable to start it only slightly faster and then to make an *accelerando* to measure 154. The fermata at the end should not be too long.

IV Sehr langsam (Very slow) 30

This piece in **ABA** form should begin quite soon after the last notes of the previous piece have ended. The tender mood requires a warm singing tone and good voicing. Play all the 32nd notes in the outer sections freely. The three fermatas in measure 11 add up to a very long silence before the lovely **B** section. The three statements of the theme are at different dynamics levels. Allow the last chord to fade almost completely and then make only a "breathing" comma before beginning the next piece.

V Sehr lebhaft (Very fast) 32

The form is **ABACBA**. Dotted rhythms and imitative writing are featured in the sprightly **A** sections, which require a light touch, fingers close to the keys, and free arms. Play the arabesques in measures 15–31 rather freely and with careful pedaling. Start the **B** section quietly at measure 52, so that the virtuosic outburst at measure 82 is a bold surprise. Make only the slightest *ritard.* in the closing two measures of the piece. One writer justly sums up this piece as representing "the 'Kreislerian' heart of the cycle: fragmentation, allusion, interweaving of characters, alternations of style, ideas without closure, distancing versus involvement, all perfectly balanced in a combinatorial art."[26]

VI Sehr langsam (Very slow) 39

This expressive piece in **ABACA** form opens with the lilting rhythm of a *siciliano*. The grace notes in the melody should be played before the beat, so that the dotted rhythm that follows is not compromised. The accent on the last chord of measure 5 should not be too strong because the following **B** section begins with a sudden *f*. Start the tender **C** section a bit under tempo. Redistributions between the hands are certainly possible in measures 27–32. The dynamic climax arrives on the E-flats in measure 32. The beauty of the part-writing in all the sections makes this piece one of the highlights of the entire work.

---

26 Antonio Rostagno, *"Kreisleriana" di Robert Schumann* (Palermo: L'Epos, 2007), 180.

VII   Sehr rasch (Very fast)

The form is **ABA** (abbreviated) **Coda**. This propulsive piece calls for extreme virtuosity, including fast rolled chords, fleet fingers, and challenging leaps. In the **A** sections, the upbeat 32nd notes in the RH must be clear and the top notes of the arpeggiated LH chords should coincide with the main beats in the RH. These chords should be "ripped" quickly, and the 16th notes in the RH played close to the keys and not overly articulated. Save maximum speed and volume for measures 71–82, and cut back to f in measure 82. The **B** section is especially difficult in measures 54–70, which could begin $\textit{mf}$ in order to conserve strength for the faster and louder return of **A** at measure 71.

VIII   Schnell und spielend (Fast and playful)

This highly effective piece in **ABACA** form calls for extremes of dynamics and a wide variety of touches. The *scherzando* character of the **A** theme (later used in the finale of Schumann's *First Symphony*, Op. 38) requires the fingers to be kept close to the keys at all times, with a light RH thumb and slight up and down motions in the wrist. The rhythmic displacements in the LH here and later need careful study, for the patterns change slightly. The effect of the opening section should be fleeting, ethereal, almost ghostly. By contrast, the **B** section presents a warmly lyrical theme in the LH in $\frac{2}{4}$ meter against the RH in $\frac{6}{8}$. Practice the hands separately for the required nuances in the LH and absolute rhythmic regularity in the RH. The **C** section is the dramatic and dynamic high point of *Kreisleriana*—grand and inexorable, using every register of the piano. The tempo can be somewhat broader, but keep the rhythm tight and the bass notes in good balance with the other voices, perhaps by half-pedaling. During the magical final descent in the closing measures, the right knee can be placed against the underside of the keyboard for good balance as the body moves to the left. There is no *ritard.* at the end, but it is effective to hold the body in place for a moment over the last staccato notes, preserving the whimsical mood for a moment. Interestingly, Schumann once advised Clara to end this piece with "a crescendo and some strong chords, otherwise there'll be no applause"—a change that he fortunately did not make in his later edition.[27]

---

27   *Complete Correspondence of Clara and Robert Schumann*, 322.

SOURCES CONSULTED

Barthes, Roland. "Loving Schumann" and "Rasch." In *The Responsibility of Forms: Critical Essays on Music, Art and Representation.* Translated by Richard Howard. Berkeley: University of California Press, 1991: 293–312.

Beaufils, Marcel. *La Musique de piano de Schumann.* Paris: Librairie Larousse, 1951.

Brendel, Franz. "Robert Schumann with Reference to Mendelssohn-Bartholdy and the Development of Modern Music in General." In *Schumann and His World.* Edited by R. Larry Todd. Translated by Jürgen Thym. Princeton, NJ: Princeton University Press, 1994: 317–337.

Daverio, John. *Robert Schumann: Herald of a "New Poetic Age."* New York: Oxford University Press, 1997.

———. *Nineteenth-Century Music and the German Romantic Ideology.* New York: Schirmer Books, 1993.

Davies, Fanny. "On Schumann, and Reading Between the Lines." *Music & Letters* VI/3 (1925): 214–223.

Hoffmann, E. T. A. *Fantasy Pieces in Callot's Manner.* Translated by Joseph M. Hayse. Schenectady, NY: Union College Press, 1996.

———. *E. T. A. Hoffmann's Musical Writings: Kreisleriana; The Poet and the Composer; Music Criticism.* Edited by David Charlton. Translated by Martyn Clarke. New York: Cambridge University Press, 1989.

———. *The Life and Opinions of the Tomcat Murr.* Translated by Anthea Bell. London: Penguin Books, 1999.

Hofmann, Renate and Kurt Hofmann. *Johannes Brahms als Pianist und Dirigent.* Tutzing: Hans Schneider, 2006.

Lara, Adelina de. "Clara Schumann's Teaching." *Music & Letters* XXVI/3 (1945): 143–147.

Litzmann, Berthold. *Clara Schumann: An Artist's Life.* Translated by Grace E. Hadow. New York: Vienna House, 1972 (1st ed. 1913).

———. *Letters of Clara Schumann and Johannes Brahms.* Edited by Berthold Litzmann. Translated by Grace E. Hadow. 2 vols. New York: Longmans Green and Co., 1927.

McCorkle, Margit L. *Robert Schumann: Thematisch-Bibliographisches Werkverzeichnis.* Mainz: Schott, 2003.

Reich, Nancy B. *Clara Schumann: The Artist and the Woman.* Revised edition. Ithaca, NY: Cornell University Press, 1985.

Rosen, Charles. *The Romantic Generation.* Cambridge, MA: Harvard University Press, 1995.

Rostagno, Antonio. *"Kreisleriana" di Robert Schumann.* Palermo: L'Epos, 2007.

Swafford, Jan. *Johannes Brahms.* New York: Vintage Books, 1999.

Schafer, R. Murray. *E. T. A. Hoffmann and Music.* Toronto: Toronto University Press, 1975.

Schumann, Clara. *Clara Schumann's Briefe an Theodor Kirchner.* Edited by Renate Hofmann. Tutzing: Hans Schneider, 2006.

Schumann, Clara and Johannes Brahms. *Clara Schumann—Johannes Brahms: Briefe aus den Jahren 1853–1896.* Edited by Berthold Litzmann. 2 vols. Leipzig: Breitkopf & Härtel, 1927.

Schumann, Robert. *Robert Schumann's Leben aus seinen Briefen geschildert.* Edited by Hermann Erler. 2 vols. Berlin: Ries & Erler, 1887.

———. *Tagebücher.* 3 vols. Edited by Georg Eismann and Gerd Nauhaus. Leipzig: Deutscher Verlag für Musik, 1971–1987.

Schumann, Robert and Clara. *Complete Correspondence of Clara and Robert Schumann.* 2 vols. Edited by Eva Weissweiler. Translated by Hildegard Fritsch and Ronald L. Crawford. New York: Peter Lang, 1994–96.

———. *The Marriage Diaries of Robert and Clara Schumann.* Edited by Gerd Nauhaus. Translated by Peter Ostwald. Boston: Northeastern University Press, 1993.

ACKNOWLEDGEMENTS

I wish to thank Donald Manildi, Curator of the International Piano Archives at the University of Maryland (IPAM) for making available early editions and historic recordings; Dr. Thomas Synofzik, Director of the Robert-Schumann-Haus in Zwickau, who shared archival material; the helpful staffs of the Library of Congress, the New York Public Library, Stanford University, the British Library, and the Royal Ontario Museum. At Alfred Music, I am indebted to E. L. Lancaster, Vice President/Keyboard Editor-in-Chief, for involving me in the project; Bruce Nelson for his engraving expertise; and Albert Mendoza for his careful and thoughtful editing. Finally, I thank William Kloss for his suggestions and patient support.

To the inspiring artist-teachers with whom I studied this work: Jorge Bolet, Béla Böszörmenyi-Nagy, Gaby Casadesus, Emil Danenberg, Stewart Gordon, and Thomas Schumacher.

Dedicated to my friend F. Chopin

Kreisleriana

Fantasies for the Piano

Robert Schumann (1810–1856)

Op. 16

I

II

Sehr innig und nicht zu rasch (Very intimate and not too fast, ♩ = 66)

(a) In measures 1 and 3, the first edition has ⟨ below the left-hand part; in the second edition, that crescendo is omitted and ⟨⟩ appears above the right-hand part.

(b)

18

Intermezzo I
Sehr lebhaft (Very lively, (♩ = 96)

Intermezzo II

Etwas bewegter (Somewhat agitated, ♩ = 92)

22

Langsamer (erstes Tempo) (Slower [Tempo primo])

½ pedal   simile

(c) The note A in the right hand has a natural sign in both editions. Clara Schumann changed it to an A-flat in her *Instructive Ausgabe* and in the *Gasamtausgabe*. This editor prefers A-flat.

III

Sehr aufgeregt (Very agitated, ♩ = 96)

(b) The *f* is placed on the penultimate eighth note in both editions, presumably an error.

(c) Alfred Cortot, Emil von Sauer, and other editors have suggested faciliations for this difficult coda. This editor suggests a redistribution following this pattern:

(d) The italicized fingering in measures 140, 141, 151 (right hand) and 159 is Schumann's.

(f) These are Schumann's pedaling indications, including three with specific releases. The editor's pedaling is chosen for reasons of sonority.

(e) Cortot's redistribution is recommended:

IV

(a) Schumann's metronome marking is ♪ = 66 and the meter is in cut time in both editions. Clara Schumann changed it to common time in her *Instructive Ausgabe* and in the *Gesamtausgabe*. This editor agrees with common time.

Bewegter (With motion)

(b) The italicized fingering in measures 12–16 is Schumann's.

V

Sehr lebhaft (Very fast, ♩ = 126)

ⓑ The slur ends at the bar lines in the second edition. This editor follows the slurring given in the
first statement of the passage (measures 72–81) in both editions.

ⓒ The E is erroneously a quarter note in both editions.

VI

Sehr langsam (Very slow, ♪ = 84) ⓐ

Durchaus leise zu halten (Very quietly throughout)

ⓐ Schumann's metronome marking

ⓑ The right-hand note on the downbeat is a G in the first and second editions. This was changed to a tied A-flat by Clara Schumann in her *Instructive Ausgabe* and the *Gesamtausgabe*, a reading with which this editor agrees.

ⓒ Schumann's fingering.

VII

Sehr rasch (Very fast, ♩ = 96)

(a) The second beat in the left hand is a C in both editions. This was corrected to a G by Clara Schumann in her *Instructive Ausgabe* but not in the *Gesantausgabe*. This editor agrees with the G.

46

VIII

(a) Arpeggio signs are omitted on the second beats in the left hand in measures 33, 37, and 41 in both editions.
Clara Schumann added them in her *Instructive Ausgabe* but not in the *Gesamtausgabe*. This editor agrees with the additions.

ⓑ This note is B-flat in both editions. Clara Schumann corrected it in her *Instructive Ausgabe* and the *Gesamtausgabe*.

© In measures 78–79 and similar measures, Schumann's notation suggests
that the hands are to be interlocked, with the thumbs overlapping.
Pianists who find this awkward may redistribute the inner voices:

ⓓ The *p* does not occur until the first 16th note of measure 126 in both editions, possibly due to the cramped space
at the end of measure 125, where it seems to belong. In any case, the dynamic has been *p* since measure 114.

ENDNOTES

The notes in this section provide a detailed listing of revisions between the first and second editions of *Kreisleriana* that may be of scholarly interest. They are compiled here to avoid excessive annotations to the score. As a reminder, the second edition contains Schumann's final intentions. Minor engraving errors have been corrected without comment. As a convenience to performers, discussion more directly related to interpretation and performance has been included in the music as footnotes.

The following abbreviations are used in the notes below:

SE   The **Second Edition** (Leipzig, 1850, Whistling) (the primary source)
FE   The **First Edition** (Vienna, 1838, Haslinger)
m./mm.   measure/measures

I (Äusserst bewegt)

m. 8: no repeat in *FE*

m. 26: ***pp*** in *FE*

m. 41, beat 2: *ritard.* in *FE* without a subsequent *Im Tempo* (*a tempo*) indication

m. 49: no repeat in *FE*

II (Sehr innig und nicht zu rasch)

m. 1: ***mf*** in *FE*

mm. 2 and 4, beat 1: ***f***, not ***sf***, in *FE*

m. 4, beat 3: ***p*** in *FE* but not in *SE*

mm. 9–10: RH part in *FE*:

m. 20, beat 3: *Im Tempo* omitted in *FE*

m. 28, beat 1: *ritard.* in *FE*

m. 31, beat 2: grace notes omitted in *FE*

m. 47, RH: third-from-last 16th note is G-flat in *FE*

m. 54: repeat omitted in *FE*

m. 56: The *Erstes Tempo* section (pick-up to m. 56 through m. 75, end of beat 2) is omitted in *FE*

m. 56: The pick-up to m. 56 is printed as 16th notes in *FE*, with no change of meter until m. 56.

m. 83, beat 1: *ritard.* in *FE*

m. 118, beat 2: *ritard.* in *FE*

m. 119: no repeat in *FE*

m. 123, beat 2: *ritard.* in *FE*

m. 126, beat 3: *ritard.* in *FE*

m. 147: mm. 20–27 repeated at this point in *FE*, with the *ritard.* in m. 20 beginning on the second beat rather than the first

m. 147: *ritard.* in *FE* but not in *SE*

m. 163: marked *Adagio* in *FE*

III (Sehr aufgeregt)

m. 31: *ritard.* in *FE*

m. 34: a *crescendo* sign spanning the entire measure in *FE*

mm. 40, 56, 65: *ritard.* in *FE*

IV (Sehr langsam)

m. 1: The first two RH chords are written *portato* () in *FE*.

m. 1: A *crescendo* sign extends from the second to the third chord in *FE*.

m. 4: **ƒ** over the G-octave grace note in *FE*

m. 4: RH accents and ⟨ in *FE*:

m. 8, beat 1: **pp** and *ritard.* in *FE*

m. 8, beat and-of-1: *ritard.* in *FE*

m. 8, beat 3: A *crescendo* extends from the grace note to the penultimate chord of the measure in *FE*. The penultimate chord is accented in *FE*.

m. 17, beat 3: *ritard.* in *FE*

m. 17, beat 4: **pp** in *FE*

m. 21, beat 3: *ritard.* in *FE*

m. 24: accents in both hands on penultimate chord in *FE*

m. 27: final cadence in *FE*:

V (Sehr lebhaft)

m. 71: *Im Tempo* omitted in *FE*

m. 160: *ritardando* over the entire measure in *FE*

m. 161: The piece ends on the dominant in *FE*:

VI (Sehr langsam)

m. 15, beat 10: accent in both hands in *FE*

m. 17: *Im Tempo* omitted in *FE*

mm. 20, 22, and 26, beat 4: *ritard.* in *FE*

m. 38: marked *Adagio* in *FE*

VII (Sehr rasch)

m. 107: *ritard.* in *FE*

VIII (Schnell und spielend)

m. 15, beat 1: *ritard.* in *FE*

m. 64, beat 1: *ritard.* in *FE*

m. 90, LH, beat 1: accent missing in both editions

m. 92, LH, beat 1: accent in *FE* but not in *SE*

m. 132, beat 1: *ritard.* in *FE*